Leaves

Preschool/Kindergarten

Save time and energy planning thematic units with this comprehensive resource. We've searched the 1990–1998 issues of *The Mailbox®* and *Teacher's Helper®* magazines to find the best ideas for you to use when teaching a thematic unit about leaves. Included in this book are favorite units from the magazines, single ideas to extend a unit, and a variety of reproducible activities. Use these foliage activities to develop your own complete unit or simply to enhance your current lesson plans. You're sure to find everything you need for "tree-mendous" learning.

Editors:
Angie Kutzer
Thad H. McLaurin
Michele M. Stoffel Menzel

Artist:
Teresa R. Davidson

Cover Artist:
Kimberly Richard

www.themailbox.com

©2000 by THE EDUCATION CENTER, INC.
All rights reserved.
ISBN10 #1-56234-363-7 • ISBN13 #978-156234-363-7

Manufactured in the United States
10 9 8 7 6 5

Table of Contents

Thematic Units...

Fantastic Fall Foliage!

ideas contributed by Katy Zoldak • Pre/K Special Education • Metzenbaum School • Parma, OH

Leaf through these activities and you'll find a harvest of fun seasonal ideas for your little ones.

Lovely Leaf Prints

Adorn your classroom with this array of colorful fall foliage. Preface this activity by taking your youngsters on a leaf-collecting excursion. Then, to make a leaf print, paint the back of a fresh leaf with brown, yellow, orange, red, or green tempera paint. Place the leaf—paint side down—on a large sheet of construction paper. Continue painting leaves and placing them on the paper until the paper is nearly covered. Lay a sheet of waxed paper atop the leaves and use a rolling pin to gently roll over them. Carefully lift the waxed paper and the leaves to reveal the print.

Autumn Leaves Banner

Youngsters can collectively create a wonderful autumn banner while working at this fun art center. In advance, cut a piece of bulletin-board paper large enough to cover a table at this center; then tape the paper to the table. Write your favorite leaf or autumn song or poem on the paper. Stock the center with markers, crayons, scissors, construction paper, leaves, and leaf stencils. In this center, a child uses the materials provided to decorate the bulletin-board paper with one or more leaf designs. Finish by removing the paper from the table, trimming it as desired, and suspending it from the classroom ceiling.

Ska-tat!

No doubt your little ones will cozy up to this fun reading experience. On a sunny fall day, take your students outside. Lay a blanket under a tree and have your youngsters sit on the blanket. Encourage them to examine the leaves on the tree or any leaves falling. Read aloud *Ska-tat!* by Kimberley Knutson (check your library). After reading the story, have youngsters collect leaves, sort them by color, and rake them in rows as the children did in the story.

Look What I Did!

Read aloud excerpts from *Look What I Did With A Leaf!* by Morteza E. Sohi (Walker And Company). Afterward have your youngsters collect many different types and sizes of tree leaves. Back in the classroom, supply each child with a large piece of construction paper and glue. Review each page in the story, showing the youngsters each leaf creature. Then encourage each student to use his leaves to create his own simple leaf animal.

Leaf Counting

This "tree-mendous" center will help youngsters practice one-to-one correspondence. Program each of five tree cut-outs with a dot set from one to five. Place the tree cutouts and 15 small leaf cutouts at a center. To use this center, a child counts each dot on a tree cutout, then places a leaf on each dot.

Classifying Leaves

Your little ones will love taking a closer look at leaves in this science center. Ask your youngsters to collect many different types of tree leaves. Attach pieces of magnetic tape to the backs of several leaves that were collected. Then, on a dry-erase board, use a dry-erase marker to make a graph. Program the left column with different types of tree leaves. In the center place the leaves with magnet strips, the dry-erase board, and a magnifying glass. Have each student examine the leaves carefully and sort them by type, placing each leaf in the corresponding space on the graph.

Leaf Rubbings

Add an autumn flair to your classroom when doing leaf rubbings. To make a rubbing, place a leaf—back side up—on a table. Place a sheet of typing or tracing paper on the leaf. Use a crayon or a colored pencil to repeatedly rub across the leaf. Repeat this process until several leaf rubbings are on your sheet. Display these bright reminders of fall foliage on a wall or bulletin board.

Explorations

Luscious Leaves

Cabbage, lettuce, spinach…these leaves are of the tasty variety. Toss up this activity so that your little ones can get a real taste of scientific exploration!

STEP 1

Label a paper-leaf shape as shown to create a graph. In advance of this activity, direct each child to wash his hands. Ask the group, "Do you think you can eat leaves?" Record each child's response on the graph.

STEP 2

Emphasize that many types of leaves should not be eaten by people, and remind your little ones that they should not eat anything unfamiliar without first asking an adult. Show the group a head of lettuce and explain that lettuce is one kind of leaf that is eaten often. Give each child a paper towel and invite her to peel off a leaf from the head of lettuce. Ask the children to compare leaves with their neighbors. How do the leaves look alike? How do they look different?

STEP 5

If your little ones are surprised to discover that some of the foods they eat are leaves, have them join you in singing this song.

Oh, I Can Really Eat Some Leaves!
(sung to the tune of "Do You Know The Muffin Man?")

Can I really eat some leaves,
Eat some leaves, eat some leaves?
Can I really eat some leaves,
When I eat my lunch?

Cabbage is a kind of leaf,
Kind of leaf, kind of leaf.
Cabbage is a kind of leaf,
That I can munch at lunch.

Lettuce is a kind of leaf,
Kind of leaf, kind of leaf.
Lettuce is a kind of leaf,
That I can crunch at lunch.

Spinach is a kind of leaf,
Kind of leaf, kind of leaf.
Spinach is a kind of leaf,
That I can eat at lunch.

Oh, I can really eat some leaves,
Eat some leaves, eat some leaves.
Oh, I can really eat some leaves,
When I eat my lunch!

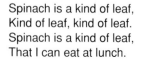

Science You Can Do

by Suzanne Moore

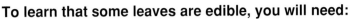

To learn that some leaves are edible, you will need:
— two green bulletin-board paper-leaf shapes
— marker
— one paper towel per child
— one head of lettuce, washed
— one head of cabbage, washed
— kitchen knife
— one bunch of smooth-leafed spinach, washed
— magnifying glasses

STEP 3

Next show the group a head of cabbage. Dramatically cut the cabbage in half so your little ones can see how tightly the leaves are nestled. Show the group the bunch of spinach leaves so that youngsters can observe that the leaves grow in clusters. Give one cabbage and one spinach leaf to each child. Ask the children to compare the three types of leaves. Provide magnifying glasses so youngsters can take a closer look at the stems and veins.

STEP 4

Encourage youngsters to taste each of the three different kinds of leaves. Record their comments on the second leaf shape.

The dark green leaf tastes _really_ green!
My cabbage is crunchy.

Did You Know?

- Some types of leaves—such as tomato-plant leaves and potato-plant leaves—are toxic when ingested.
- Leaves make food for a plant.
- A leaf's veins carry food and water in the leaf.
- Many grazing animals and other animals—such as koala bears, giraffes, and elephants—depend on leaves for their food supply.
- Many food products come from leaves. The leaves of the tea plant are used for tea. The oil from peppermint and spearmint leaves is used to flavor gum and candy. Leaves such as bay, sage, and thyme are used to flavor foods.

What Now?

Invite your little ones to help you make this delicious snack using three types of fresh leaves—lettuce, dill, and basil.

Leafy Roll Ups

Scoop eight ounces of soft cream cheese into a large mixing bowl. Add two tablespoons of lemon juice, one-fourth cup of chopped fresh dill, and one-fourth cup of chopped fresh basil to the cheese and mix well with a mixer. To make one treat, spread some of the cheese mixture on a large lettuce leaf. Roll up the leaf, and munch!

"Tree-mendous"

A multidisciplinary unit on trees and leaves

by Lucia Kemp Henry

We Need Trees

Leafy trees are very important for the health of our environment. Share some of these interesting facts with your students so they can develop an appreciation for how much we really need our leafy neighbors.

- Trees take in carbon dioxide. In return, they give off the oxygen that people breathe.
- Trees cool the air. They allow water to evaporate from their leaves, which cools the air around them.
- Because the hairy leaf surfaces of trees trap and filter dust and pollen, they reduce air pollution.
- Trees reduce noise pollution by acting as natural sound barriers.
- Tree roots prevent erosion.
- For wildlife, trees are a source of food and shelter.
- Trees provide cool shade for protection from the sun on hot days.
- Trees produce foods, such as fruits and syrup.
- Trees reduce the velocity of strong winds.
- Trees make our world a beautiful place to live by camouflaging unsightly things, by varying their color, and by producing beautiful blooms.

Learning Centers With Leaves

Quickly create some practical centers, using the leaf patterns (page 15).

- Duplicate two copies of the leaf patterns on page 15. Cut out each leaf design and glue it to tagboard card. To use the cards for a Concentration-type game, have students place them facedown and attempt to turn over matching leaf pairs.
- Number the leaves on a copy of the leaf patterns; then cut out the leaves and glue them to tagboard cards. To use these leaf cards, have students arrange them in numerical order.
- Cut out copies of the leaf designs and glue them to tagboard cards. Cut each card in half. Mix up the card halves. To use the cards, have students find the matching halves.
- Duplicate the leaf patterns in a variety of colors. Cut out each design. Glue several leaf cutouts to each of several sentence strips to establish patterns. To use these pattern strips with a supply of loose leaves, have students manipulate the leaves to repeat or continue each pattern.

Leaves Everywhere

Use the basic leaf patterns (on page 15) to create a variety of art projects, games, and classroom decorations. Reproduce the leaf patterns, enlarging them if desired. Cut out the leaves and have your students complete their choice of the following projects:

- Decorate construction-paper headbands with the leaf cutouts.
- Cut the center from a paper plate. Glue leaf cutouts around the plate rim to make a decorative wreath.

- Lightly sponge-print each leaf with a contrasting color. To make a classroom tree, glue or tape the painted leaves to a bare tree branch secured in a large container.
- Border a bulletin board with sponge-painted leaf cutouts.
- Create a leaf-shaped nametag to be worn on a field trip to a local nursery or tree farm.

Fall Splendor

Red Leaf, Yellow Leaf by Lois Ehlert (Harcourt Brace Jovanovich, Publishers) is perfect for introducing tree information to young children. Read the book aloud and discuss each of the collages. Share some of the factual information found at the back of the book. If possible, display real leaves, buds, roots, bark, and seeds of a maple tree. Then encourage each student to make leaf artwork for display. To make red and yellow leaves, finger-paint one sheet of finger-paint paper red and another yellow. When the paint is dry, trace an enlarged maple-leaf shape (pattern on page 15) on each sheet. Cut on the resulting outlines. Collect the leaves painted by your students, and tape them on and around a tree cutout to create a huge tree full of bright fall foliage.

Changing The Perspective

Trees can be special in many ways. This lovely book celebrates all the things a tree can be. After reading aloud *Hello, Tree!* by Joanne Ryder (check your library), take your youngsters outside or visit a local park. Ask students to locate a big, leafy tree. Ask them to lie down on towels in a big circle under the tree, so that their feet are toward the tree's trunk and they can clearly observe the tree's canopy. Encourage each youngster to say a word that describes something about the tree. Jot down the students' descriptions of the tree.

Classifying Leaves

Just as Joanne Ryder's *Hello, Tree!* (check your library) points out, tree leaves come in many shapes and sizes. Ask your youngsters to collect many different types of tree leaves. Divide students into several small groups, and give each group a variety of leaves. Assist the students in each group as they sort their leaves according to similar characteristics. For example, students may sort their leaves by shape (round, skinny), by color (red, yellow), by texture (smooth, rough), or by size (large, small). Have youngsters glue several samples of each category of leaf to a large sheet of paper. Before putting the papers on display, label (or have students label) each with a category.

A Sorting Center

After your little ones have made the booklets described in " 'What Grows On Trees?' Booklet," they'll enjoy this classification game (page 14). Draw a simple picture of a tree. Label the picture with the words "leaves," "fruit," and "flowers" as shown. Then duplicate page 14, and then color, laminate, and cut out the classification game cards. Place the cards and the tree picture in a learning-center area. To use the center, a student places each of the cards under the appropriate heading to indicate whether it is a leaf, a fruit, or a flower.

"What Grows On Trees?" Booklet

As each youngster compiles his own tree booklet, he'll explore answers to the question, "What grows on trees?" Duplicate the booklet cover and pages (see pages 11–13) on white construction paper for each youngster, and cut apart the pages. If full-size booklet pages are desired, enlarge each booklet page design using a photocopier; then make multiple copies. Begin by asking each child to color his booklet cover and personalize it. On page one of the booklet, have each student glue one or more real or paper leaves in the available space, before coloring the remainder of the page as desired. To complete his copy of booklet page two, ask each student to color as desired, then glue crumpled balls of tissue paper or add sponge-print shapes to represent flowers. On page three, have each child draw fruit (or attach fruit stickers) before coloring the page. To complete page four of the booklet, ask each student to draw people, animals, birds, or insects who benefit from the life of the tree. As each student dictates, write his completion for the incomplete sentence on booklet page five. Assist each youngster in assembling his booklet.

Tree Hotel

Help your youngsters understand the importance of trees as homes for animals with this fun activity. Begin by reading aloud *Tree Trunk Traffic* by Bianca Lavies (check your library). This photograph-illustrated book introduces some familiar animals that depend on trees for protection. Discuss how the tree helps each animal.

Draw a simple picture of a tree, complete with canopy, trunk, and roots. Label the picture with the words "The Tree Hotel." Label the roots, trunk, and canopy with the words "basement," "first floor," and "top floor" respectively. Ask students to name animals that might live on each floor of their tree hotel. For example, worms, lizards, and skunks might live in the basement of the tree, while raccoons and birds inhabit the first floor, and other birds and squirrels have the run of the top floor. Have students draw or cut out pictures of animals and glue them to the appropriate areas of the tree.

Tree Things Collage

Organize a nature hunt to collect tree twigs, leaves, and seeds. Also ask your youngsters to collect these things from their yards at home. Once your collection has reached a suitable size, have your students sort the collection into three different boxes labeled "twigs," "leaves," and "seeds." Starting with a large sheet of construction paper, have each youngster glue on his choice of items from your collections to make a collage. Display all of the collages on a bulletin board titled "Twigs, Leaves, And Seeds."

Tiny Trees

This simple craft project will give each of your little ones an opportunity to create a tiny tree for a tabletop display. On white construction paper, duplicate the canopy and trunk patterns on page 16. Cut out the canopy design, and paint or sponge-paint it on both sides. Cut out the tree trunk pattern. To create a barklike effect, place the trunk pattern on top of a piece of crumpled paper bag or on tree bark before coloring it with the side of an unwrapped crayon. Roll up the tree trunk cutout and glue the ends together where indicated. Cut slits along the broken lines. Insert the tree canopy in the trunk by sliding it into the slits. Have each student display his tree on a tabletop with those of his classmates. Encourage youngsters to add small plastic animals to the display and use it to role-play life in the forest.

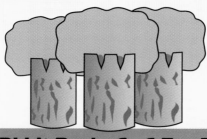

Did It Begin As A Tree?

Display several objects such as a pencil, a book, a T-shirt, an apple, a metal can, a wooden toy, a plastic toy, a box of tissues, a small plastic milk jug, and a carrot. Hold up the items one at a time, and find out whether students believe a tree was involved in their production. After discussing tree-related products, explain to students that anything made of wood or paper started with a tree. If possible, show students a fallen tree, a stump, or a cross section cut from a log, so that they can see the wood beneath the tree's bark. Afterwards, have students sort groups of objects to indicate whether or not they were made from or came from a tree.

"Tree-mendous" Reading Material

Crinkleroot's Guide To Knowing The Trees
Written & Illustrated by Jim Arnosky
Published by Bradbury Press

Hello, Tree!
Written by Joanne Ryder
Illustrated by Michael Hays
(Check your library.)

The Oak Tree
Written & Illustrated by Laura Jane Coats
(Check your library.)

Once There Was A Tree
Written by Natalia Romanova
Illustrated by Gennady Spirin
Published by Dial Books For Young
     Readers

Red Leaf, Yellow Leaf
Written & Illustrated by Lois Ehlert
Published by Harcourt Brace Jovanovich

Tree Trunk Traffic
Written & Photographed by Bianca Lavies
(Check your library.)

The Tremendous Tree Book
Written by May Garelick and Barbara
     Brenner
Illustrated by Fred Brenner
Published by Four Winds Press

Booklet Page 1

A tree has leaves.

Booklet Cover   Use with "'What Grows On Trees?' Booklet" on page 9.

My Tree Book

by _____

Booklet Page 3

A tree has fruit.

Booklet Page 2   Use with " 'What Grows On Trees?' Booklet" on page 9.

A tree has flowers.

12

The best thing about trees is...

©The Education Center, Inc. • *Leaves* • Preschool/Kindergarten • TEC3176

A tree has friends!

©The Education Center, Inc. • *Leaves* • Preschool/Kindergarten • TEC3176

Classification Game Cards

Use with "A Sorting Center" on page 9.

Leaf Patterns

Use with "Leaves Everywhere" and "Learning Centers With Leaves" on page 8
and "Fall Splendor" on page 9.

redbud

maple

oak

elm

hoptree

tulip tree

Tree Patterns
Use with "Tiny Trees" on page 10.

finished project

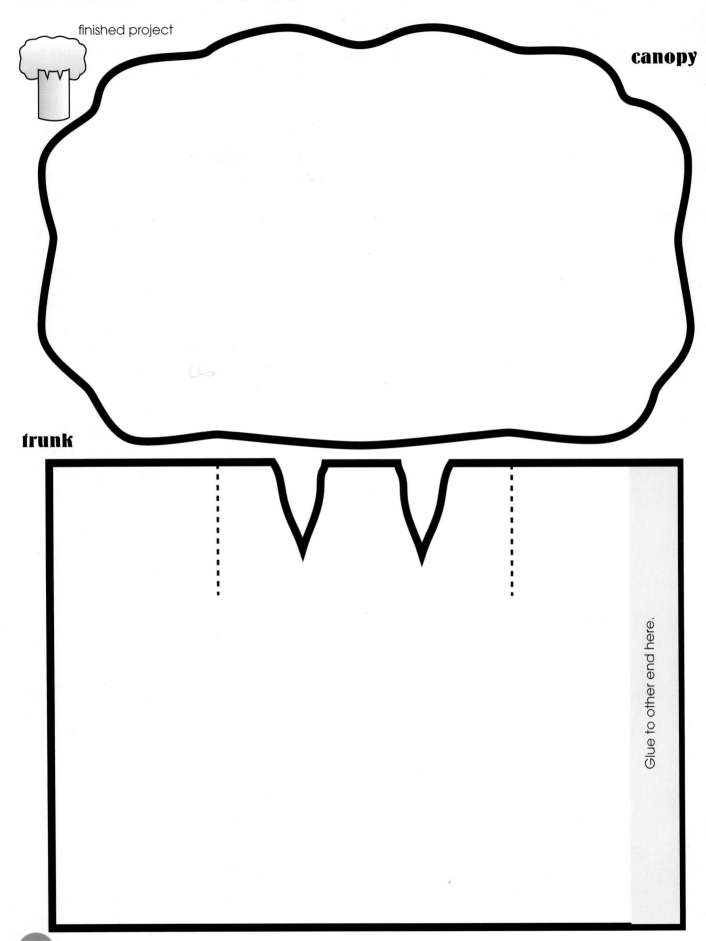

canopy

trunk

Glue to other end here.

Autumn's Dancers

Leaf through this unit to find easy science activities focusing on students' observation, classification, comparison, and inference skills. Then breeze through a movement activity, our reproducible science booklet, and art activities.

by Lucia Kemp Henry

Leafy Patterns

In this introductory activity, guide students in observing that leaves, like dancers, are not all alike in appearance. Display several leaves from the same tree or plant. Ask students if the leaves look the same or different. Take away all but one of the leaves. With it, display three new leaves, all from different trees or plants. Ask students if the leaves are the same or different. As students focus on the leaves, have them describe the differences in shape, size, and color. Then have students complete the visual discrimination and patterning activity on page 20.

Leaf Sorting

Take your youngsters on a leaf-collecting excursion. Then, using the activity sheet on page 21 and the leaf cutouts on page 22, have students classify leaf cutouts into two groups—*wide* and *narrow*.

Foliage Features

In this circle activity, students study two leaf attributes simultaneously. Prepare for this exercise by cutting out and laminating red, yellow, and blue construction paper duplicates of the leaf patterns on page 23. Place two Hula-Hoops in the middle of the circle so that they overlap. Put a question-mark cutout in the area shared by both circles, and label each remaining section with an attribute. For example, have students examine the leaf cutouts to locate ones that are red and/or circular, before placing them in the appropriate Hula-Hoop sections. Help students conclude that leaves in the overlapping section must be both red and circular. Repeat this activity with several attribute combinations.

Plant Pals

This simple science experiment demonstrates the importance of plants in our environment. Have students use a magnifying glass to closely examine a well-watered, potted plant's leaves; then discuss what they see. Place a clear, rigid plastic bag over the potted plant. Tie the bag off to completely seal it. Set the plant in an indoor sunny location. The following morning, have your students discuss what changes have occurred. *(Water droplets have formed on the bag.)* Where do students believe the moisture came from? *(The plant's roots pulled the water from the soil, through the stem and leaves, where it was released into the air—and condensed on the bag.)* Since your students can see that leaves release water into the air, how do they think leaves can help the environment? Help them conclude that leaves add moisture to the air and aid in cooling the earth. Also explain that leaves give off oxygen, filter pollutants, and shade animals in streams and rivers.

"Lotsa" Leaves

Reproduce pages 24, 25, and 26 on white construction paper and cut on the solid lines. Tear or have students tear light green, dark green, red, orange, yellow, and brown construction paper into small bits, keeping bits separated by color. Then have students color and decorate each page as indicated. Staple the pages into booklets, and discuss the changes in the trees.

Directions For Completing Booklet
Cover—Draw and color leaves around the title. Or glue small construction paper leaf cutouts around the booklet title.
Page 1—Glue dark green construction paper bits to the tree branches.
Page 2—Glue red, orange, and yellow paper bits to the tree branches.
Page 3—Glue a few red, orange, and yellow paper bits on the tree branches. Then glue more on the ground.
Page 4—Glue red, orange, and brown paper bits on the ground around the tree trunk.
Page 5—Glue light green construction paper bits to the tree branches.

Fashionable Foliage

Here's a hat that's worth dancing about. Make a tagboard, leaf-shaped cutout using the pattern on page 27. On large sheets of art paper, have students finger paint or spatter paint using red, yellow, and orange paint. When this artwork is dry, trace (or have each student trace) the leaf outline onto the paper three times, and cut out the

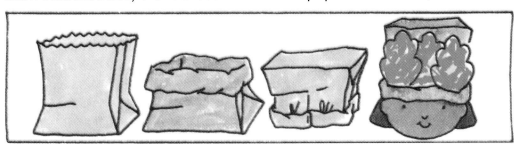

resulting leaf shapes. Beginning with a medium-sized brown grocery bag, fold down the rim two or three times to form a hat brim. Glue three leaves to the front of the bag hat. Take a tuck or two in the back of the bag to adjust the fit for the wearer. Staple in place.

Whirl and Twirl

Watch your youngsters whirl and twirl as they impersonate windblown leaves. Set the stage for this movement activity with appropriate instrumental music such as Beethoven's Symphony Number Six, "Pastorale," or a selection by pianist George Winston, or one by harpist Andreas Vollenweider. As your youngsters twirl to the melodies, describe moments in the life of a fall leaf to stimulate the students' expressive movements. You might describe, for example, a leaf attached ever so precariously to a branch—twisting first one way, then the other. Or describe a leaf tumbling end over end across a meadow. Whatever the mental pictures your youngsters call to mind, they'll no doubt enjoy expressing them in movements.

Leafy Patterns

Leaves are different.
Look at each row.
Color matching leaves alike.

Find the missing leaves.
Cut, glue, and color.

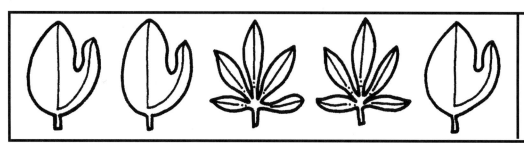

Note To Teacher: Use with "Leafy Patterns" on page 17.

Name_____

Leaf Sorting

Some leaves are **wide.**

Some leaves are **narrow.**

 Cut and glue the leaves.

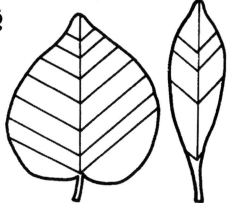

These leaves are **wide.**	These leaves are **narrow.**

©The Education Center, Inc. • *Leaves* • Preschool/Kindergarten • TEC3176

Patterns   Use with "Leaf Sorting" on page 21.

Award

_____

has learned a lot about
leaves.

Ask him or her
to tell you about them
sometime.

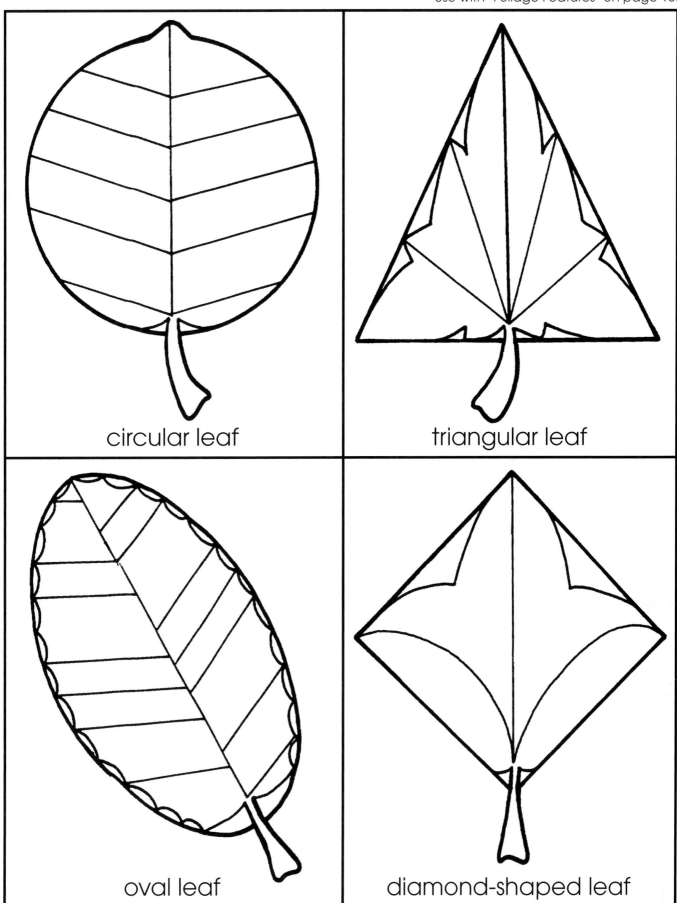

circular leaf

triangular leaf

oval leaf

diamond-shaped leaf

Leaf Booklet

Use with "'Lotsa' Leaves" on page 19.

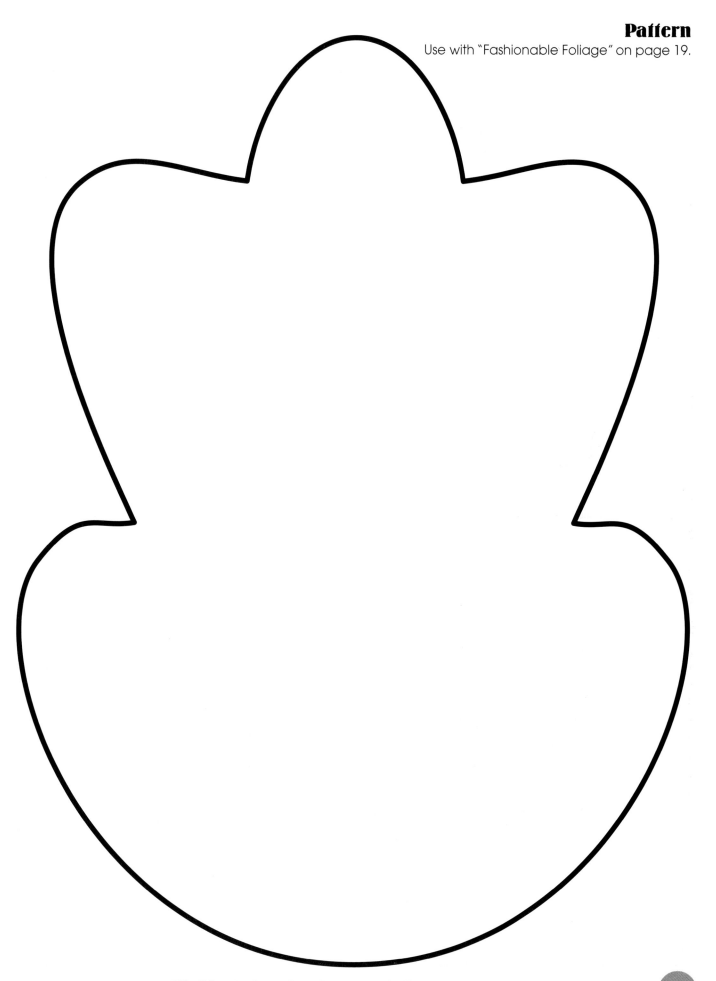

Wonders Never Cease

Falling For Leaves

Leaf through this colorful collection of hands-on science activities. Then choose your favorites and invite your youngsters to jump right in. You'll have bushels of fun!

by Lori Bruce

Pam Crane

Activity 1

You will need:
brown lunch sacks (one per child)
freshly fallen leaves
white construction-paper squares
glue
bulletin board paper

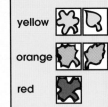

What to do:
   Give each youngster a lunch sack. Take youngsters outside and ask them to collect freshly fallen leaves and place them in their sacks. Bring youngsters back inside. Then have them remove their leaves from their sacks and examine them.

Questions to ask:
   1.   What do you notice about the leaves?
   2.   Why aren't all of the leaves the same?

Then:
   Have each youngster glue his favorite leaf onto a construction paper square. To create a graph, program a length of bulletin board paper similarly to the one shown. Then have each youngster glue his square to the appropriate section of the graph.

Questions to ask:
   1.   How many leaves are red (yellow, orange)?
   2.   Which color has the most (the least) leaves?

Activity 2

You will need:
a variety of freshly fallen leaves
red, yellow, and orange paint
paintbrushes
poster board squares (two per child)
pencils

What to do:
   Have each youngster personalize the backs of two poster-board squares. Then, to create a leaf print, have each youngster paint the underside of a leaf and press it onto the front of one of his squares. Have the youngster make an identical print on his remaining square. When the prints are dry, store them in a basket. A youngster matches two squares, then turns them over to check. Youngsters can also use the squares for seriation activities.

Questions to ask:
   1.   What do you notice about the shapes of the leaves?
   2.   Why do you think the leaves are different shapes?

This is why:

Leaves are different sizes, shapes, and colors. In the fall, shorter days and cooler nights cause chlorophyll (a green pigment) to break down. The leaves then show their yellow, orange, red, or purple pigments.

This is why:

Each kind of tree has its own special kind of leaves. Deciduous trees (trees that shed their leaves) have leaves that are smooth, toothed (like maple leaves), or lobed (like oak leaves).

Activity 3

You will need:
one-inch coffee filter strips (one per child)
pencils
freshly picked green leaves
Popsicle sticks (one per child)
a jar
rubbing alcohol

What to do:
Have youngsters personalize the tops of coffee filter strips. Then have each youngster position a leaf horizontally across his strip about two inches from the bottom. Using a Popsicle stick, have each youngster gently rub his leaf to transfer some of its pigments onto his strip. Pour rubbing alcohol into the jar so that it is about one inch deep; then have each youngster insert his strip into the jar. Leave the strips in the jar for about 30 minutes; then have youngsters remove them and set them aside to dry. Discard the alcohol.

Questions to ask:
1. What do you see on your strip?
2. Why do you think the streak is yellow?

This is why:

A green spot and a yellow streak formed on the strip. Leaves contain several color pigments. As the alcohol moved up the strip, it dissolved and separated the green and yellow pigments. When we look at a leaf, we see the green pigment, chlorophyll, because there is more of it. Other color pigments are present, too, but they are masked by the chlorophyll. In the fall a leaf stops producing chlorophyll and we can see its other color pigments.

Activity 4

You will need:
an assortment of freshly fallen leaves
waxed paper
crayon shavings (in fall colors)
newspaper
an iron
scissors
a hole punch
monofilament line
small twigs (one per child)

What to do:
Have each youngster arrange several leaves on a sheet of waxed paper, then add a sprinkling of crayon shavings. Place a second sheet of waxed paper on top of each youngster's creation; then place the sheets between layers of newspaper. Press the sheets together with an iron set on medium. Remove the sheets from the newspaper and let them cool. Have each youngster cut loosely around each of his leaves and punch a hole in the top of each cutout. Help each youngster tie each of his cutouts to a twig with a length of monofilament line; then suspend his mobile from the ceiling.

To follow up this activity, discuss composting with your youngsters. Then have youngsters take any leftover leaves back outside and place them in the woods or in a nearby compost pile.

Questions to ask:
1. What are some things people do with leaves in the fall?
2. What do you think happens to leaves that fall in the woods?
3. What is composting?
4. Why do you think people should compost leaves?

This is why:

In the fall people may rake, blow, or burn leaves. Leaves that are left in the woods begin to be broken down into simple substances that provide food for plants. People should compost leaves because it saves landfill space and makes food for plants.

"Tree-mendous"

Letter Leaves

Read aloud Leo Lionni's *The Alphabet Tree*. Then get your youngsters busy making leaf prints or rubbings. Have each student cut out a print or a rubbing and write a letter of the alphabet or a sight word onto the leaf. Have each youngster attach her leaf to a paper tree branch mounted on a bulletin board. This attractive display will be a great reminder of the letters or words that youngsters have learned.

Richelle Kreber and Sharon Roop—Gr. K
Slate Hill Elementary
Worthington, OH

Where Does That "Leaf" Us?

Now that it's autumn, there are plenty of leaves floating around. With this movement activity, there will also be plenty of skills floating around, such as following visual directions and increasing the ability to focus. In advance, draw a visible arrow on a large, leaf-shaped cutout. Prepare two smaller leaf cutouts for each child. Laminate the leaves for durability. When you are ready to begin, tape leaf cutouts to each child's palms. Ask students to show their leaves moving up; then show them the large leaf with the arrow pointing up. Then ask students to show their leaves moving down and show them the same leaf, this time with the arrow pointing down. Continue the experience by asking children to move their leaves up or down, based on the direction of the arrow. Leaves up, leaves down—movement skills, all around!

Leaf Ideas

The Leaves Are Falling Down

Ask each child to fingerpaint a leaf cutout using his choice of red, orange, yellow, or brown paint. To make necklaces, punch a hole and thread a length of yarn through the top of each leaf. Have youngsters wear their necklaces. Encourage each child to spin around and "fall" to the ground when the color of his leaf is sung.

(sung to the tune of "The Farmer In The Dell")

The leaves are falling down.
The leaves are falling down.
Red, orange, yellow, and brown.
The leaves are falling down.

Amy Ubelhart—Preschool
Lil Bumpkins Daycare
Shavertown, PA

If Feels Like Fall

Give youngsters a feel for fall by encouraging them to feel and describe a real tree's trunk and freshly fallen leaves. As a follow-up, have little ones make artistic fall trees. Glue torn, brown construction-paper strips onto a large sheet of finger-painting paper to resemble the rough trunk and branches of a tree. Randomly drop spoonfuls of different colors of liquid tempera paint onto the paper. Cover the paper with a large sheet of waxed paper; then press and rub the paint. Allow the paint to dry completely; then peel away the waxed paper. Cut around the shape of the tree and its brightly colored, leaf-filled branches. Now it feels *and* looks like fall!

Bernadette Hoyer—Preschool
Coles and McGinn Schools
Scotch Plains, NJ

Falling Leaves

This smooth, soft autumn song gives little ones practice with slow and controlled movement. Before adding motions to the song, discuss the movement of leaves and how leaves might be affected by the wind. As a music extension, use a set of bells or an Autoharp® to help children hear the downward movement of the melody. Encourage them to show this downward movement with their bodies as they dance freely to the song.

Leaves are fal-ling down.
Slow-ly to the ground.
Some are gold. Some are brown.
Nev-er make a sound.

Dr. Grace Morris
Southwest Texas State University
San Marcos, TX

Leaves Are Falling Down

Leaves are fal- ling down.

Slow- ly to the ground.

Some are gold. Some are brown.

Nev- er make a sound.

A Nature Swim

If walking through a pile of autumn leaves is not an option at your school, take little ones on a "nature swim" inside the classroom. Fill a small wading pool with dry leaves that you've collected. Then invite youngsters to walk through the leaves, listening to the crunchy sounds and smelling the aroma of autumn.

Doris Porter—Preschool
Headstart
Anamosa, IA

Cascade Of Colorful Leaves

As a tribute to the season, fill your room with these cascading leaf art projects. Duplicate several brown construction-paper copies of a spiral design. Also supply colorful leaf designs. If desired, have youngsters collect leaves. To make a cascade, cut out the spiral design. Then glue the leaves to the spiral, and suspend it by a thread from the ceiling.

Nancy Knutson
Oakview Elementary
Osseo, MN

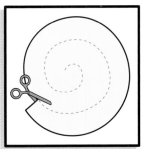

Leaf Toss

Whirling, swirling leaves will leave your little ones all aflutter! So will this group movement activity that requires a flurry of cooperation. Space your children evenly around a large sheet or a parachute. Instruct each child to hold the sheet tightly with both hands. Place a supply of real leaves or decorative fabric leaves (from a craft store) in the center of the sheet. Challenge the group to move the sheet slowly at first, then faster until all of the leaves have flipped up and floated to the ground. Ask the group to put down the sheet, gather the leaves, and begin again. Whee!

Susan Burbridge—Four-Year-Olds
Trinity Weekday School
San Antonio, TX

Fall Leaves

Your youngsters will love the colorful effect of these appealing fall leaves. To make a leaf, pinch the end of a spring-type clothespin and insert a cotton ball. Dip the cotton ball in yellow, orange, green, or red powdered tempera; then rub it on a piece of manila paper. Repeat this process several times overlapping colors, until the paper is completely covered. Shake the excess paint from the paper. Place the manila paper on a sheet of newspaper. Using a water-filled spray bottle, mist the paper. When the paint is dry, trace a tagboard leaf cutout on the paper. Then cut on the resulting outline. Mount the leaves on a wall or bulletin board for a great fall display!

Deborah Zumbar—Pre/K
First Presbyterian Preschool
Alliance, OH

Colorful Foliage

Bright and beautiful leaf art is a snap to create using this technique. Place a red, orange, or yellow crepe paper leaf cutout on white art paper. Securely hold the cutout in place as you gently paint over the crepe paper with a wet brush. (Be careful not to use too much water on the brush.) Carefully remove the crepe paper leaf to reveal the bright impression beneath. Repeat this process several times, using different colors of crepe paper.

Take A Closer Look!

Encourage hands-on learning and lots of discovery opportunities at this science center. Provide acorns, a variety of leaves, twigs, pinecones, pieces of tree bark, and magnifying glasses at a table. Also supply paper, crayons, and markers. While in this center, a child uses the magnifying glass to carefully examine the objects. She then draws her scientific observations on paper.

Five Little Leaves Fingerplay

Your little ones will enjoy the movements suggested for this little leaves fingerplay. As a variation, die-cut five leaf shapes to create a flannelboard set for use with the rhyme. Or hold leaf cutouts in front of an air-conditioning unit. At the appropriate points in the rhyme, let go of one leaf at a time so the children can watch the "wind" blow it to the ground!

[Five] little leaves up in a tree;
They're as bright as they can be.
Along comes the wind blowing all around,
And one little leaf falls to the ground.

Stand up; hold up five fingers.

Make wind sound. Shake fingers.
Crouch down; touch floor.

Shelley Hoster—Two- And Three-Year-Olds
Jack & Jill Early Learning Center
Norcross, GA

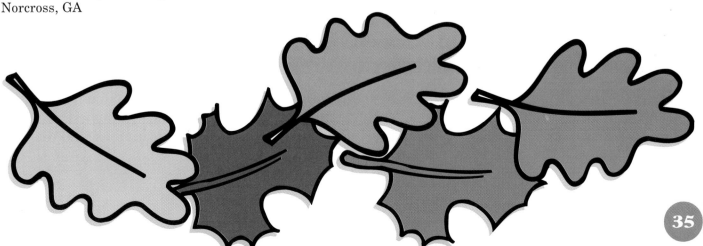

Bringing The Outdoors Indoors

If your class has adopted a nearby tree to observe for the year, use this yearlong display idea to bring it to life indoors as well. Wrap a large section of white bulletin-board paper around the tree's trunk at the children's level. Have students work together as they use brown crayons to fill the paper with tree rubbings. Before returning inside, have each child pick up one of the tree's fallen leaves; then instruct him to make a rubbing of his leaf when he returns to class. Cut around the resulting leaf shapes; then cut a tree shape from the tree rubbing. Attach the tree to a classroom wall and add each child's leaf rubbing to its branches. As the students observe the tree's changes outdoors, be sure to reflect those changes on the indoor tree as well. What a "tree-mendous" opportunity for learning!

Tammy Bruhn—Pre-K
Temperance, MI

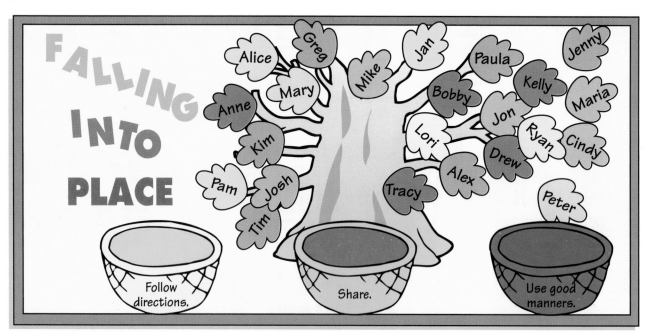

This colorful autumn display is sure to communicate your high expectations. Label several baskets or basket cutouts with classroom goals. Mount the baskets on a board along with a title and a tree cutout. Personalize a supply of colorful leaf cutouts with students' names, and display them randomly on the tree's branches and across the board.

Elaine J. Swindell, Providence Preschool, Swan Quarter, NC

Leaves Are Falling All Around!

Take youngsters on an outdoor leaf hunt. Or have them hunt for construction-paper leaves hidden around your classroom. Follow up your leaf hunt with this fingerplay that teaches the sign-language symbols for *red, yellow, orange,* and *brown*.

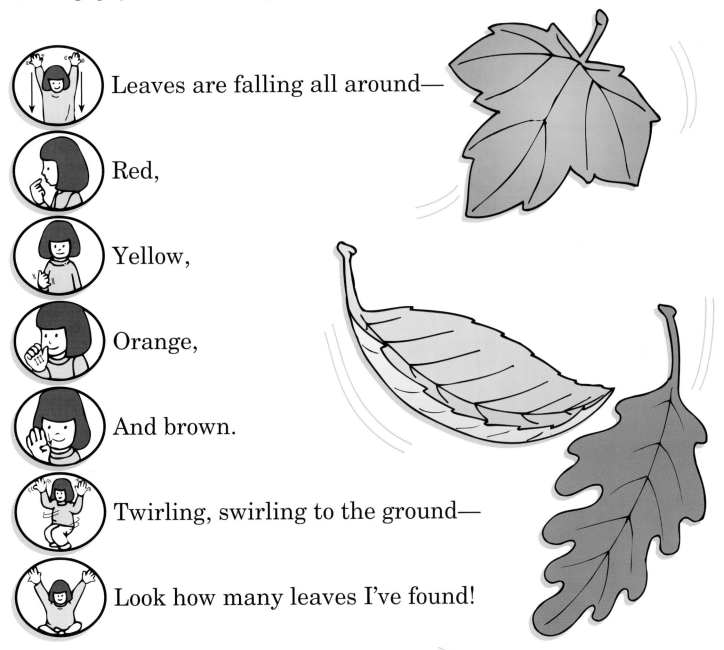

Leaves are falling all around—

Red,

Yellow,

Orange,

And brown.

Twirling, swirling to the ground—

Look how many leaves I've found!

—*Jan Trautman*

Fall Foliage Mobile

Your little ones will love the colorful effect of this work of art. To make a leaf mobile, arrange a fresh leaf on a sheet of waxed paper; then add a sprinkling of crayon shavings. Place a second sheet of waxed paper on top of the crayon shavings; then place the sheets between layers of newspaper. Press the sheets together with an iron set on low heat. Remove the waxed paper sheets from the newspaper and let them cool. Next cut loosely around the leaf and punch a hole in the top of the cutout. Personalize each cutout and tie it to a leafless tree branch with a length of fishing line. Suspend this mobile from the ceiling for a colorful fall display.

Leaf Batik

Sample the colors of fall with this art exploration. Have youngsters collect an assortment of freshly fallen leaves. Then place a large piece of cardboard on a tabletop and cover it with a piece of muslin cloth. (Provide a small cloth piece to make an individual wall hanging, or have the children work cooperatively on a large cloth piece to use as a background for a fall-themed bulletin board.) Have a youngster choose a few leaves to arrange atop the muslin. Invite him to pound the leaves with a wooden mallet, causing the leaves' colors to bleed onto the cloth. My, the leaves are lovely this time of year!

Marsha Feffer—Four-Year-Olds
Bentley School, Salem, MA

Autumn Is Here

Have each child tape die-cut leaves to a length of yarn or clear fishing line. Then invite him to whirl and swirl his leaves while singing this autumn song.

(sung to the tune of "Have You Ever Seen A Lassie?")

> The leaves are really changing,
> And changing, and changing.
> The leaves are really changing,
> For autumn is here.
>
> See red leaves and brown leaves,
> And green leaves and gold leaves.
> The leaves are really changing,
> For autumn is here!

Linda Rice Ludlow—Preschool, Bethesda Christian School
Brownsburg, IN

Reproducible Activities...

Additional Materials Needed For Each Child

— 30-inch length of yarn
— 2 plastic drinking straws
— blunt needle
— scissors

How To Use Page 41

1. Duplicate page 41 on construction paper for sturdiness.
2. Have children trace the shape of each leaf and acorn and color all the pieces; then cut them out on the bold lines.
3. Instruct children to cut the straws into one-inch sections.
4. Finally, direct children to lace the paper shapes on the yarn, using the needle to poke a hole in each shape as they go. (*You may decide to provide prethreaded needles.*) Form spacers by inserting the straw pieces between each paper shape to give the necklace better support.
5. Tie the yarn ends together to form a necklace.

Finished Sample

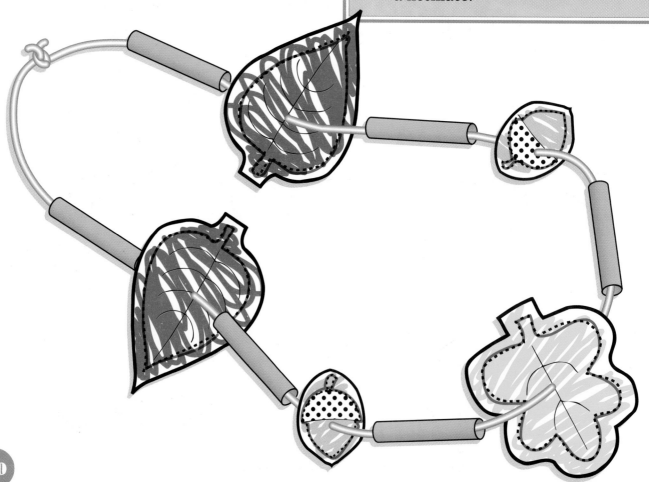

Name _____

Autumn Treasures

 Trace.  Color.

Cut.

Lace.

Foliage Basket

How To Use Page 43

1. Duplicate page 43 on construction paper for sturdiness.
2. Have the children color the basket and handle and then cut them out.
3. Fold the basket on the dotted line.
4. Staple the handle along the leaf-and-acorn border.
5. Staple the remaining open side together.
6. Use the basket while on a fall walk to collect fall leaves, acorns, and other items.

Finished Sample

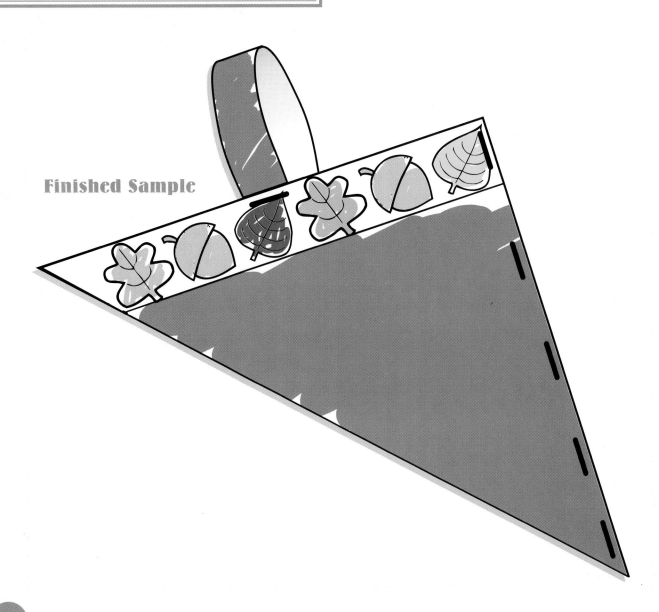

Basket Of Beauty

 Color. 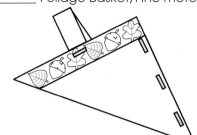 Cut on bold lines.

Fold. Staple.

Staple.

Staple.

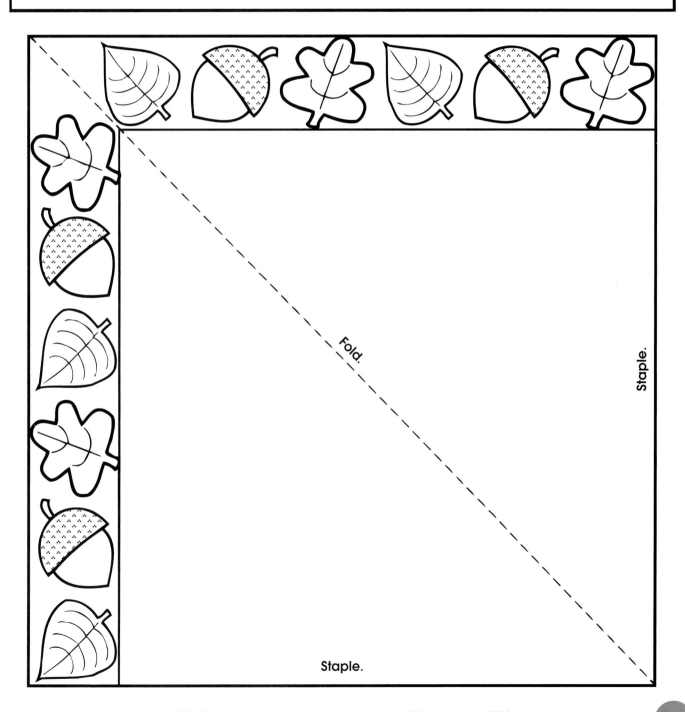

Fold.

Staple.

Staple.

Name _____

Kitties In The Leaves

Color the leaves in each row that are the same.

Name _____

Tree Twins

Color the leaves that are alike.

Laughing Leaves

 Cut and  glue to match the shapes.

  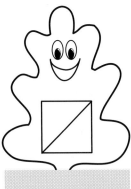 

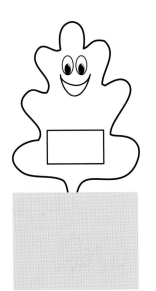   

©The Education Center, Inc. • *Leaves* • Preschool/Kindergarten • TEC3176

Name _____

Leafy Letters

Find letters that are alike.

🖍️ Color those sections.

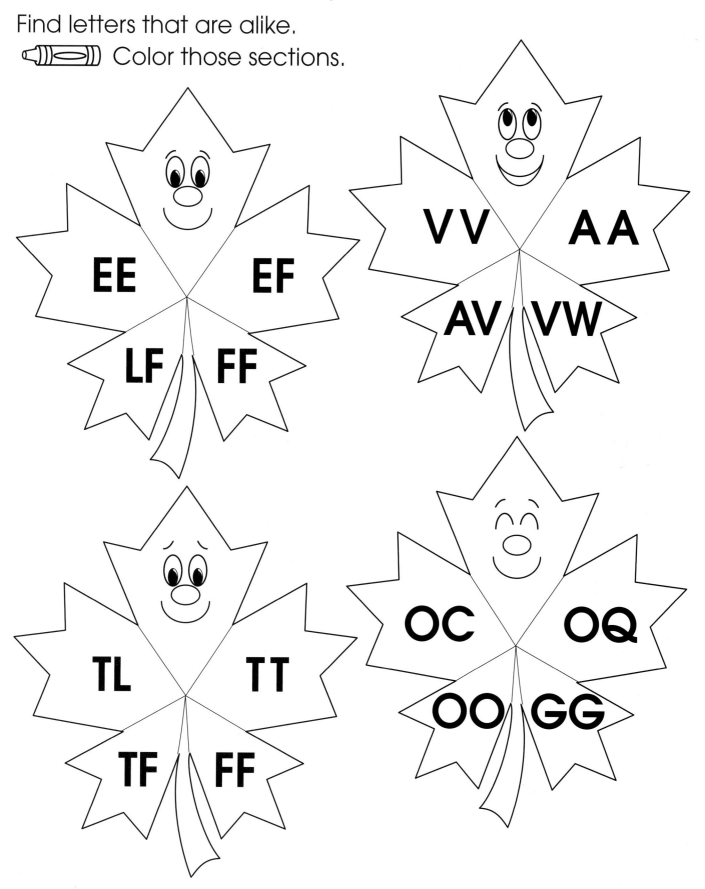

····Leafy Activity Cards····

How To Use This Sheet

   1. Duplicate the page several times on construction paper.
   2. Color the leaves; then laminate the page.
   3. Use a permanent marker to program the leaves with the matching skills of your choice. (For example, program half of the leaves with numerals and the other half with corresponding dots.)
4. Cut apart the cards.
5. To do this activity, a child matches each leaf card to a corresponding card.

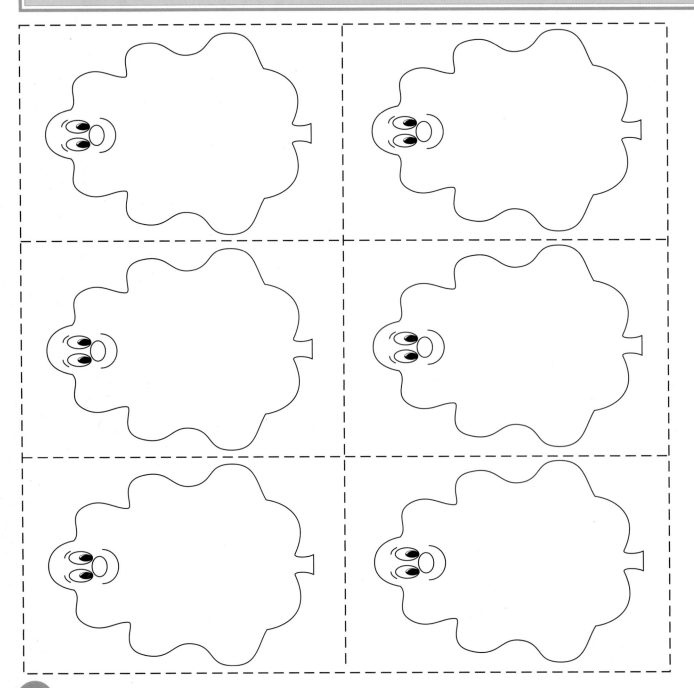